ROOSTER
The Diary of a Puli Puppy

Jacki Evans

Published by Jacki Evans
Publishing partner: Paragon Publishing, Rothersthorpe
First published 2015
© Jacki Evans 2015

Illustrations: Isobel Quill

The rights of Jacki Evans to be identified as the author of this work have been asserted by her in accordance with the Copyright, Designs and Patents Act of 1988.

All rights reserved; no part of this publication may be reproduced, stored in a retrieval system, or transmitted in any form or by any means, electronic, mechanical, photocopying, recording or otherwise without the prior written consent of the publisher or a licence permitting copying in the UK issued by the Copyright Licensing Agency Ltd. www.cla.co.uk

ISBN 978-1-78222-430-3

Book design, layout and production management by Into Print
www.intoprint.net
+44 (0)1604 832149

Printed and bound in UK and USA by Lightning Source

I OWE A GREAT DEAL OF THANKS to Helen, who made me see I can do anything I set my mind to;
To Pete for his enthusiasm and encouragement;
To generations of Hungarian Pulis, all of whom taught me something else about this wonderful breed;

And lastly of course, to Rooster himself, a puppy in a million, who gives me so much love, laughter and unlimited *Puli Kisses*.

1: IN THE BEGINNING

Hello everyone, my name is Rooster. I am a Hungarian Puli puppy and I live here in the country, near a town called Kington, in England with my Puli mummy and daddy, my granny who is very old and some other Pulis who are all my relations and one other dog who is called Wilma and she is a Hungarian Pumi.

There are also two humans who live with us and take care of us, they are called Mum and Dad and I love them very much.

When I was born I shared a lovely big warm bed with my two sisters and my brother.

The first thing I remember is opening my eyes and being able to see my mummy. I had been able to see light for just a little while but now I could actually see. I crawled around to her face and she looked at me and smiled and said "Hello my beautiful baby" then she gave me lots of kisses. I snuggled up to her and went back to sleep. My brother and sisters hadn't opened their eyes yet, so for a while I was able to make it to the milk bar much quicker than the others but gradually over the next couple of days they caught up with me.

We were soon trying to walk, at first we had to concentrate very hard to get our tummies off the ground. I found I could manage a couple of steps and then over I would go but I was very determined and after a few days of practice I got the hang of it.

It was still a bit hit or miss for all of us for a while I remember, one of us would manage to toddle over to another, lift a paw to give him a smack and over we would go again. But you would be surprised how quickly we learnt to control our little legs. By the time we were about three weeks old we were having such a wonderful time, playing and rolling around in our big box with a lovely soft blanket underneath us and lots of toys. At first we couldn't work out what was a toy and what was a puppy but we soon learned to recognise each other.

For the first few weeks mummy stayed cuddled up to us all the time but gradually as we got bigger she began to leave us to play although she popped in several times a day to feed us and make sure we were clean. We soon became big, fat, contented babies. Our Mum and Dad were around a lot too, only at first we didn't know who they were, but we soon got used to them stroking us and lifting us up for cuddles.

As we grew bigger we were moved from our box in the bedroom into a lovely big pen downstairs which was full of our toys and we could run and play and roll each other over and we could see everything that went on in the house. Sometimes we would fight, growling at each other and biting ears and tails but it was never really serious and then we would all be friends again.

When we were very little we all thought we would just stay here with our family forever but our daddy who is called Hank and is quite old and a very wise daddy explained to us that it is the job of nearly all baby Pulis to leave home when they are big enough and go and live somewhere else. He told us that if this didn't happen lots and lots of people would never know the joy that a Puli in their family would bring them, which would be just *SO* sad. It is our job to go and spread Puli love and kisses all around the world. Our daddy told us a story of when he was a baby puppy and he was put in a box and onto something called an aeroplane and he was brought here from a land far away called America. Can you believe it? He said he had been a bit scared at the time but his daddy who was called Sprout had told him that he must be brave and it would all be okay in the end. When he got to England Mum and Dad were there to meet him and they loved him very much and he loved them and this is what happens. So Reba, Polly, Artie and I are looking forward to when we go and spread Puli love and kisses to other families. But we hope it might be without the aeroplane bit.

A few weeks ago Mum loaded us into our crates in the back of the car and we went for a ride to see a man called a vet. I think this man was very important. We were taken into a dark room and he shone different lights in our eyes, it seemed to take a very long time but we were very good puppies and kept really still. When he turned the light back on he said we were all clear and he told us what good puppies we had been and that we all had beautiful eyes.

It seemed silly to take us all that way when anyone could have told him we have beautiful eyes. Still we gave him some Puli kisses to show that we liked him too.

Then just a little while after that visit we heard that we had to go to the vet again and were looking forward to seeing the important man who liked our eyes but we were not in the car so long that time and the place we went to was different. This man was also very nice at first, he stroked us and told us we were beautiful (of course). He looked in our ears and mouths and listened to our hearts with what looked like some kind of toy on a string, but then, can you believe it he stuck a needle in each of us. It was a bit of a shock and it stung a bit as well but there were some nice ladies there who gave us cuddles and kisses and we were soon feeling better.

After that we concentrated on learning to be good puppies for when we would be ready to go to our new homes. We tried to remember only to do our business outside in the garden and we learnt to stand very still to have our collars put on and then to walk on a lead – we all became quite good at this as long as the person holding the lead went in the direction we wanted to go. We didn't cry or bark at night, but this could have been because we were together, I was never quite sure how we would feel when the time came for us to be on our own, but I knew, as always, we would try to be good.

2: MY BROTHER AND SISTERS LEAVE HOME

As we grew older a lot of people began to visit us, some were friends of my Mum and Dad and had just come to play with us. My daddy says it is so we get used to seeing people we don't know and don't get frightened. Mind you I think my daddy is a big show-off as when people do come to see us he makes a big fuss of them and rolls on his back and waves his legs in the air. We can hardly get a look in. Some of the people seem to spend more time than others, just looking and playing with us and the rest of the family and Mum and Dad spent a long time talking to them about Pulis and asking them a lot of questions.

One day a nice lady and man came and after playing with us all they took my sister Polly away with them in their car. It was strange without her and then the very next day a lovely family with a little boy came and took Artie. This did feel odd and a bit sad but Reba and I cuddled together that night and I made up stories for her about the lovely new homes Polly and Artie had gone to and how much they will be loved. After that Reba and I stayed together for quite a long time. We played and raced each other around the garden and had just the best time.

Then this week Mum gave us both a bath. What is it with humans and baths? We had already had one and we thought that once it was done it was another thing that had to happen to puppies and could then be forgotten about. But no! I asked daddy about it and he just said "You have to get used to it son, it's a fact of life". Anyway, just because I had rolled Reba over in the mud and got pretty muddy myself, in the bath we went. I was quite good because I now realise that that Mum is not trying to drown me, which is what I thought the first time. But I STILL don't like the big machine that blows hot air and growls at me. When it was all over and we were dry, we looked really pretty and smelled good too.

The next day while we were playing some more visitors arrived. We made a big fuss of them and gave them lots of Puli kisses because we LOVE visitors and they liked us very much. But after a while my Mum picked me up and took me back to our pen without Reba and do you know what? I haven't seen Reba since! I waited for Mum to bring her back to our pen but she never arrived. Eventually Mum came and let me out. I looked everywhere for my sister but she just wasn't there. I was *SO* upset but Mum and Dad made a big fuss of me and gave me a new Teddy and a new chew bone and after a while we went into the garden and played chase with a tennis ball. So I was kept quite busy until bedtime.

I was very lonely then though, there was a big space next to me, where Reba should have been and I missed her *SO* much. I have to tell you that I did have a little cry just for a while, I was *SO* lonely. But Mum had put a lovely thick soft blanket in the crate and I had my new Teddy with me and best of all one of the two snuggle blankets that Reba and I had had in our bed, which I could smell her on, so eventually I was a good boy and went to sleep. I found out that the other snuggle blanket went with Reba to her new home, so I know when she went to bed the first night she could smell me. I hope she wasn't too sad or unhappy on her own.

    I asked daddy the next morning why Reba had to go away and he told me she had a very important job to do. It seems that the lovely family who came to see us had had a Puli who was 16 years old! Can you believe that? 16! Granny is only 13 and she is ANCIENT! Anyway for some reason their Puli went away, daddy didn't tell me where she went but I heard him say something to mummy about the Rainbow Bridge, anyway this family were so sad because they missed their Puli very much and they had no one to give them Puli love and kisses. So Reba has gone to live with them and fill their house once more with Puli love and kisses and make them happy again.

3: NEW ADVENTURE

The most important thing I have to tell you this week is that we have heard from Reba, although her name is now Luna. She is very happy in her new home, with lots of toys to play with and a human family that love her to bits. I am so happy for her. Her new mum sent us some pictures.

I have had a very busy week as Mum has been taking me to lots of new places. At the beginning of the week I had a play date with another puppy, his name was Dudley and I was very surprised to find he wasn't a Puli. He was quite strange looking and told me he was a Rot-something. When we first met he shouted at me, so loudly that I hid underneath the bench my mum was sitting on. But a boy has to be brave, doesn't he? So after a while I decided to shout back and THAT put him in his place! He really is only a baby and younger than me and after that we had a lovely game.

When I got home I was too sleepy even for my tea, I slept and slept and slept. Later when I told my daddy about my adventure playing with the Rot-something and how surprised I had been, he explained that not all dogs are lucky enough to be born Pulis and although naturally we feel sorry for them, it shouldn't be held against them. He pointed out that Wilma who lives with us is clearly not a Puli as she has long legs, big ears and whiskers, but it's not her fault and we just don't talk about it.

My other big adventure this week was going to a place where there was a big grass space and lots of people. I am still trying to work this one out. Most of the people there had white clothes on and a lot of them were rolling balls around. Mum and I sat on one of the benches to watch and a lot of people knew my Mum and came to talk to her and of course to me and gave me plenty of cuddles and kisses. What was strange is that Mum has recently taught me a really good game where she throws a ball and I chase it and bring it back to her, so although there were no other dogs there I thought this is what we had come to play. But no, when I tried to jump on the grass to fetch one of the balls, she said NO and I had to sit quietly next to her. Luckily Mum had remembered to bring my Teddy so I wasn't bored.

Then a lady who looked very important blew a whistle very loudly and the people who were on the grass came off and all the other people with the white clothes on went on to the grass. I was very confused but really excited to see my Dad was one of the people who had come off the grass. He was really pleased to see me and gave me a big cuddle. We stayed for a while after that and it was fun to watch. When I got home I was quite sleepy again and quite forgot to ask my daddy if he knew what it was all about.

For my next adventure we are going to something called *Ring Craft Classes* because Mum says I have a lot to learn. When I find out what it is all about I will let you know.

4: TRYING TO HELP MUM

Now I know this will be deeply troubling to all my friends but this week, oh dear, I can hardly say it! – I got into *TROUBLE!* Of course I don't need to tell you that I didn't mean to do wrong. I thought I was helping.

It all started when I was helping mum hang out the washing on the line. It's a fun thing to do, I choose what to hang up and Mum takes it off me. Well eventually, after a lot of laughter I think she realised I shouldn't be working so hard at my age and she lifted the basket up onto the table in the garden so I couldn't reach it. I wondered off to play on my own. Now there is a thing in our house that lives on a shelf in the kitchen and sometimes it rings. When it does someone has to go and talk to it. I was just wondering if a butterfly might be edible when the thing rang. So, telling me to be a good boy, Mum went inside to talk to it.

That is when my problems started! While I was watching the butterfly I looked up to the sky and thought it was getting quite dark, in fact I am sure I felt a raindrop on the end of my nose. This is bad news because Mum does not like her washing getting wet, so as she was still talking to the thing on the shelf, I realised it was up to me to save the washing. Now I am very little and that washing was high but I jumped higher and higher until I managed to catch hold of a blanket. At first it wouldn't come off but I hung on tightly and then *pop, pop, pop,* those pegs went flying in all directions.

Unfortunately, the blanket fell on top of me so it took a while for me to find my way out and then when I did I was left with the problem of getting it into the house. This was a very BIG blanket so first I tried to fold it so I could carry it inside. Well that didn't work as I just kept tripping over the horrid thing. It was about this time when I began to wish I hadn't tried to help and to make it worse, the sun was shining and it hadn't started to rain after all. However, I have heard my Dad say I am a determined little thing, who doesn't give up easily and I *SO* wanted to make Mum and Dad proud and get that bad blanket in for Mum. After trying a couple of different ways I found that if I took a firm hold on it then walked backwards, pulling with all my might it moved along – *hooray*!

I was about half way across the lawn when Mum came out. Oh dear, the look on her face was NOT good. I honestly thought she would be *SO* proud of me, but she wasn't, she was very cross. Well, I am not going to tell you what she said because I am only a baby and I don't think people should say those words in front of a baby. I left her to it and went into the house to tell my Teddy all about it and *SULK*!

Still, everything was okay in the end though, Mum came in and gave me a cuddle and a kiss and do you know what? I could see she was trying not to laugh. She said after all that effort I should go in my crate and sleep for a while and she was quite right; as soon as Teddy and I settled down, off I went to sleep. I couldn't help remembering though how good it was when those pegs went pop, pop, pop and flew through the air and reminded myself that when I woke up I should go and see if Mum had missed any. They do make excellent things to chew!

5: OUT AND ABOUT

On Saturday Mum and Dad took Wilma and me to a show, *wow* it was such fun. By now I am used to going to my ring craft class and out and about on my walks and I am amazed by how many different types of dogs there are from itty bitty Chihuahuas to huge Pyrenean Mountain Dogs and big tall Great Danes. But at this show there were dogs I had never seen before. There were three really enormous dogs a bit like my friend Snow who is a Pyrenean but two were black and one was black and white. I also couldn't believe my eyes when I saw a little dog that only had hair on top of his head and around his feet! The rest was just skin! What can have happened to him? He must get *SO* cold when the sun isn't shining. I expect all these different types of dogs secretly wish they had been born Pulis but of course not everybody is so lucky so I am sure they just make the best of it.

Anyway, I enjoyed myself *SO* much, the only disappointment was, although I tried *SO* hard I didn't win one of those lovely ribbony things they were giving, can you believe that? Not one!!!! There was no class for the most helpful puppy, which I am sure I would have won, nor was there a class for the prettiest puppy which I probably would have won as there were no other Pulis there, so I had to go in Handsomest Dog, Waggiest Tail and something about the dog the judge wants to take home.

I am glad I didn't win that one as although she was

a very nice lady, I didn't want her to win me and take me home with her. It would have been nice though, to win just one pretty ribbon. I was a bit sad but my Dad gave me a hug and said I was the handsomest, waggiest puppy there and he certainly wanted to take me home, so that made me happy again.

The next day we went back to the place with the big lawn where people roll balls about. I am learning about this place now as we have been quite a few times. Sometimes Dad is playing and we go to watch him and sometimes we all go together to watch other people. Anyway, now I know that they are not balls but bowls. I still don't understand why they roll them around so they crash into each other but it's a good place to go as everyone knows me now and just about everyone loves me. This time when Mum took me for a walk around I found a very tiny bowl which I brought back to our seat and rolled up and down the path for a while. Unfortunately I got a bit enthusiastic and threw it in the air, whoops! It jumped over the little wall and landed on the grass with the big bowls. I thought I might be in trouble but the lady who was playing nearest to us picked it up and brought it back for me. She said if ever they change the rules and include puppies she would certainly teach me to play. We had a big cuddle and I gave her some Puli kisses then she went back to rolling the bowls around.

6: SNAKES AND STUFF

Now I know some of you Pulis out there want to start finding things you can do to help your Mum and Dad, especially my nephew Bruin... ha ha ... that still makes me giggle, he is *SO* much older than me, and my friend Parker and some of the other Puli friends I have made on Face Book.

Well one of the things I really love is gardening. I always go with my Mum and Dad if there is any gardening to do. There is so much I can help with from picking up and taking away empty flower pots to digging holes for Mum to plant pretty flowers in. The other day I helped my dad plant potatoes. We put them in a big sort of sack and covered them with earth. When we had finished Dad said that soon we would be enjoying some lovely home grown potatoes but I think he has made a big mistake as that was at least three days ago and although I have had a close look several times a day and even digging down into the earth to see if anything is happening, there just isn't anything growing.

But there is one really important thing I want to talk about, and this is where you can help your Mum and Dad. In our garden we have a *HUGE* Water Snake. He is green and very, very long. He spends most of his time wound around a wheel against the wall, but every so often, usually when it's hot, Mum or Dad get him out and drag him around the garden where he puts water on the flower pots. I think this is

VERY silly as he is clearly a very dangerous snake, so I make it my job to always go with him and I remind him *EVERY* time, in no uncertain fashion that I have my eye on him and *ANY* attempt to hurt my Mum or Dad will be dealt with *MOST* severely and I won't hesitate to bite him HARD. I can do this now as I am losing my baby teeth and getting some really good big ones. Occasionally I just give him a bit of a nip, just so he doesn't forget! So you could have a look around your garden to see if you have a water snake lurking somewhere and if you have, make sure he knows you are watching him and who is boss. Nobody hurts our humans when we are on guard, do they?

The other thing I promised I would tell you about is my ring craft lessons. Now there might be one or two baby puppies out there that will be taken to these classes when they are a bit bigger and might be worrying about it. Well, I promise you, you don't need to be worried, they are such fun and I will explain to you what you have to do. When I get to my class which is in a hall, I have some time to say hello and play with my friends, some of them started at the same time as I did and we are always glad to see each other. I have a special friend who is about the same age as me, he is called TJ and is a Lhasa Apso. After we have had a few minutes to greet each other the very nice lady who is in charge calls everyone out and we start to learn what we have to do if we are going to go to shows.

First your Mum or Dad lifts you onto a table and you must stand still. I am used to that bit, it is easy. Then the nice lady who is pretending to be a judge comes and looks in your mouth and at your teeth and sort of strokes you by running her hands all over you. You will find this a bit difficult as it tickles a bit and it's hard to stand still when the lady is so close to you that you could give her a big kiss, but you must. Then, when she is finished, your Mum or Dad lifts you down onto the floor and you have to walk nicely down a long mat away from the lady then turn around and walk back. When you get back to her you jump up as high as you can to get a big cuddle. It is really quite simple. She also explained to our Mums and Dads that it doesn't really matter if we are going to go to shows or not as it is good for pups to learn to stand on a table to be examined by a vet for instance and also to learn to walk quietly on the lead.

    I was very proud last week as we had a new little girl join us, her name is Mishka and she is quite small and very pretty and a little bit shy. She is only 12 weeks old and is a Tibetan Terrier. Of course all the other puppies wanted to go and make friends with her but her Mum came and sat next to us and asked my Mum if Mishka could follow me as I was so good and such a happy little boy. I nearly BURST with pride. So while we were waiting to start I explained to her what we would be doing and when we went into the ring I walked really carefully so she could keep up with me and when we sat down to wait our turn I sat very close to her so no one could frighten her. I think she was happy to have me look after her. I hope she is going to be there every week.

7: THE SHOW

Last weekend, Mum and Dad took Wilma Pumi and me to another show. I don't think it was a dog show, although there were lots of dogs there but also all sorts of other animals too. It was a lovely day with the sun shining and it seemed like everybody had decided to come to this show, there were *SO* many people. Dad parked the car in a big field with all the other cars and we had our leads put on and I was lifted down. Show off Wilma jumps down by herself but she has much longer legs than me and is much older. So we set off for a walk around. Wilma was a bit worried at first, she is a bit of a scaredy cat (or dog) but I told her to stop being silly and just follow me, so she soon settled down.

Our first stop was next to a ring which had a lot of silly looking ducks in it. Now I have seen ducks before when we have been to the park but these looked very different. Luckily, because I do like to know these things, I heard someone say they were Indian Runner Ducks. Just as I was wondering if I could go into the ring to see them up close, a man walked in with a dog. I knew it was a Border Collie as I have seen one at my Ring classes. Well, the man shouted out *"Away"* and blew a whistle and off the dog went. Boy did he make those silly ducks run! Round and round they went, through some straw bales, around some poles, over a little bridge and all the time the man was whistling and shouting commands. I got quite excited and had to be spoken to about barking. Finally the dog chased the silly ducks right up into a trailer. What fun! I did hope the man might have asked if any other dogs wanted a go at chasing the silly ducks, I *SO* wanted to have a go, but sadly he didn't.

We carried on walking, there was so much to see. We stopped to watch some men with a rope. Now, there was a group of them at one end and another group at the other end. When someone blew a whistle all the men started shouting and pulling backwards, sometimes one lot managed to pull the others forward a bit then it went the other way; people were shouting for their favourite group of men. It went on for quite a while, back and forwards until one team pulled a bit more and dragged the others over a line. Then they all fell down on the grass and people started cheering. It was a bit like when Wilma and I play tug of war with our rope toy, except the ones that won didn't start running around the grass with the rope and jumping up and down like I do when I win.

We carried on, through the crowds.

It was about now a bit of a misunderstanding arose. I am sure all of you Pulis out there know that there are some small people in the world. We don't have any in our house, so until I started going out on my lead with Mum and Dad I didn't know much about them. Of course I know now because we see them in the park and other places. I think these small people are like the puppies of humans and like puppies they come in all sizes, from some nearly as big as their Mummies and Daddies to some really tiny ones. I believe they are called children and I assume you buy them somewhere but as we don't especially need one in our house, it's not something I have thought about much.

Anyway, it was very crowded and there were huge amounts of these children around. I was walking with my Dad, just a bit ahead of Mum and Wilma, when a very small one came towards us with her Mummy and Daddy. She really was not much bigger than me and she was holding something which I just knew was food, it smelt wonderful and just as she went past me she held it out to me. I *PROMISE* you she did! So, being the polite little Puli I am of course I took it, it was delicious, all creamy and cold. I was just remembering that I had to say thank you to her when my mouth wasn't so full when she started to shout, *"THAT DOG HAS TAKEN MY ICE CREAM!!!!!! THAT BAD DOG HAS TAKEN MY ICE CREAM!!!! NAUGHTY DOG HE IS EATING MY ICE CREAM!!!!!"*

What a noise she made and she kept on at the top of her voice. By this time quite a lot of people had started to stare at us, it was *VERY* embarrassing. I tried to explain to Dad that it was all a misunderstanding but the problem was that these small people can communicate with Mums and Dads much better than we puppies can and with her still shouting THAT BAD DOG HAS EATEN MY ICE CREAM nobody seemed to understand me. My Dad was offering to get the child another ice cream but luckily the child's Mum and Dad didn't seem too cross at all and said "Not to worry, these things happen" and they headed off, with her still shouting, back to the ice cream stall to buy her another one. Huh, you notice no one bothered to ask me if I would like another, and they are really good. By the way, I looked around for my Mum and she was staying back out of the way AND she was laughing so much at me she could hardly stand up! She said it was the pink ice cream around my nose and whiskers. Not my colour apparently.

After all the excitement Dad thought we should move away and go and watch something else so decided that we would watch the trotting races. Now this *IS* fun. There is a huge field marked out like a roadway and 5 horses pulling funny looking sort of carts a bit like show trollies but with only two wheels and a driver sitting on top. Well, they all line up together and a car with bars at each side drives along in front of them quite slowly. The horses run after the car which then lifts its bars and whoosh the horses go past running faster and faster.

They started over the other side of the ring but I could feel the thumping on the ground and hear the people cheering so I just had to put my feet up on the fence to watch. They were coming closer and closer, it was *SO* exciting, you could feel the ground shaking and then suddenly *flash* they had gone past us and nearly disappeared. I wanted to race after them, but of course I wasn't allowed to. What FUN it would have been sitting in the trolley racing around the field. Sometimes I think puppies are not allowed to do anything exciting!

"... all creamy and cold"

We watched two races and then carried on walking. By this time I was getting a bit tired, it had been a busy day. Mum and Dad said it was nearly time to go home but Mum just wanted to look at the chickens which were in a big tent, which dogs were not allowed in. So Wilma, me and Dad waited outside for her. Wilma was just telling me that we used to have chickens at home before I was born but a nasty fox or something came and killed them all (I wish I had been there then, I would have chased the nasty old fox right away) when suddenly "... *THERE IS THAT BAD DOG WHO STOLE MY ICE CREAM ... HE ATE MY ICE CREAM ... BAD DOGGY!!!*"

Yes Dad said, it was definitely time to go home!

8: ROOSTER AND HIS FRIEND PARKER'S BIG ADVENTURE

I woke up this morning feeling all happy and content, I had been dreaming about playing with my Teddy and other toys in the garden with the pretty flowers and how much I loved my Mum and Dad, when suddenly I felt movement like I was swaying back and forward. I could also hear a strange sort of whoosh noise and I am sure I can smell salt? Salt? Oh my *GOODNESS*, I opened my eyes as I remembered where I was! Oh *HELP!* I was on a SHIP, the bad ship Black Sheep to be precise – a Puli pirate ship ruled by the dreadful Captain Black Jack Sparrow.

It all started when my friend Parker and I were enjoying a little holiday at the seaside. We had had our breakfast, paddled in the sea, had some fun chasing seagulls on the sand and we were just walking along the shore eating our ice creams that were given to us by a very nice man in an ice cream van, when we spotted a cave deep in the rocks. Well, we are adventurous little Pulis, so finishing our ice creams we trotted over to take a look inside. Wow! It was full of wooden chests some locked and some left open so we could see gold coins and jewellery all spilling out. We both decided that it would be best to get out of there fast and try to forget all about the money and jewels. We ran out and along the sand as fast as our legs could go. Suddenly a boat pulled in full of Puli Pirates shouting "Avast Landlubbers" and "Pieces of Eight" and strange stuff like that, and we were bundled up and thrown in the boat and rowed out to the Black Sheep. We had been *Puliganged!* Since then poor Parker and me had been forced to swab the decks and climb the rigging and we had been fed on nothing but bread and water, not even an old bone.

I was just thinking how on earth were we ever going to get home when the second in command, a one eyed old seapuli called Short John Bone Apart (Shorty to his friends) threw open our door and shouted "Ha, avast me hearties, up an at 'em, get swabbing." (I really did wish we could understand the language they spoke.) We were still very tired and hadn't had our bread and water breakfast but we had to get to work straight away. Parker started swabbing the decks and I was told to go up the rigging to watch for ships. I had only just settled down when I saw a ship on the horizon. I was so frightened I shouted "Help! There's a ship over there" only to be growled at by Captain Black Jack Sparrow for using the wrong words. For a moment my mind went blank, what is it I was told to shout? Oh yes, SHIP AHOY! After that all the Puli pirates started running around and barking, and running out the cannons and shouting things like, *to me, to you, to me, to you, forward a bit, back a bit* – it all got VERY confusing. Then guns started firing at us and Parker and I got so frightened that we went below and hid in our hammocks. The firing went on for a very long time and I think we fell asleep.

When we woke it had all gone quiet and we decided we should go and find out what had happened but once again our door was flung open and a very elegant Afghan hound in velvet clothes and a big hat with a curly feather swept into the room and in a very posh voice said "Oh, two more pirates ... and these are hiding."

Quickly we tried to explain that we had been *puliganged* and we weren't pirates at all. But no one seemed to want to listen to us. The posh Afghan said "His Majesty's Navy has only one answer to Pirates, especially cowardly ones who hide when everyone else is fighting. They must walk the plank."

Now I was really scared, I don't think I can swim! I was also trying not to cry because it all seemed too much for a baby puppy. Parker, being older, was trying to keep a stiff upper lip but I could see that he was worried too. Two smaller Navy dogs, I think they were Whippets, bundled me up and stood me on the end of the plank, then they started prodding me with their bone daggers, which had been sharpened at the ends, to make me start walking. There was nothing else I could do. As I walked, I remembered my lovely life with Mum and Dad and all my family. I hoped someone would take care of my Teddy and love him as much as I do and I wondered who would protect my Mum and Dad from the Green Garden Water Snake.

By now I was at the end of the plank, I just knew I had to be brave so I shut my eyes, swallowed a little sob and jumped! I fell down and down and down. Just as I expected to hit the water I realised I must have fallen onto something soft, and whatever it was smelled pretty good too. For a minute I was too frightened to open my eyes, but decided I couldn't just lie there.

Puliganged

I carefully opened one eye and to my surprise saw something that looked very like my Teddy. I opened the other eye and, Oh Joy! I was in my own little bed, in my own crate, with my Teddy and there was my Dad saying "Good morning Rooster, would you like to go out?"

I was home! It had been a DREAM! Heck, was I HAPPY! I dashed out into the garden to check that everything was where it should be. What a wonderful day it was going to be, but I had better not eat any more of the special CHEESY Ruby Dooby Biccys before bed tonight. I really don't like those sort of adventures.

9: TEDDY'S HORRID DAY

PLEASE can anyone out there tell me is there somewhere you can report cruelty to Teddies? There surely must be somewhere? It all happened, just a couple of days ago. I was doing my rounds of the garden looking for interesting things to collect and checking out the pretty flowers when I thought to myself that my Teddy would like to be out in the sun too, so I went in to fetch him. It was strange but he wasn't in our crate where I usually leave him. Hmm, I thought, where could he be? My first stop was that naughty auntie Glory Be, she is always stealing my toys, so I went to search her basket. I found my Monkey, my Sheep, and my little Fox (she always wants my little Fox) but no Teddy. I did a quick check around the house. No, still nothing. Where could he be? Then I remembered, he had been helping me that morning to dig a bit of the America tunnel, which is behind the big fir tree. Oh heck, I left him in the tunnel!

For those of you who don't know, I am going to America to meet my friend Teddy. This may confuse you but he is a Puli who has the same name as my Teddy and lives in America with his Mum and his brother Moe. He invited me to visit and has started digging at his end. We are going to meet in the middle and he is going to show me America and I am going to visit some of my other Puli friends who live there. I think I must be close now as I have been digging for four days.

Anyway, silly me, I left Teddy down the tunnel. I raced off to fetch him but no, he wasn't there either! Where on earth could he be? Then a movement caught my eye and I looked up. Oh my goodness there was my Teddy, hanging from the washing line by his EARS!!!!!! Who could have done that? Who could be so CRUEL? Poor Teddy! I raced up to rescue him but although I jumped and jumped and JUMPED until I was exhausted I just couldn't reach him. Poor, poor Teddy, how could anyone do that? He is not a bad Teddy, he is a good Teddy. He is never naughty. I had to find someone to help me. First I looked for my Mum and tried to explain to her but she just said not now baby, I am busy, we will play later. Then I went in search of my mummy and daddy. Mummy just smiled and said silly boy and daddy gave that kind of woof noise he makes when he is trying not to laugh at me (he thinks I don't know). I even tried ancient Granny Martha but she just said "Who are you, did you bring me a biscuit?" She's hopeless!

By this time I realised that I had been away from Teddy for quite a long time, so I went back to tell him I hadn't given up, and can you believe it, he had gone? Now where could he be? *I WANT MY TEDDY!!!!* Well, I am sure you can understand that by this time I was thirsty and tired so I decided to go back to my crate for a drink of water and a quick rest before I started searching again. When I got there I couldn't believe my eyes. There, in our crate was my Teddy. I was *SO* happy I kissed and hugged him. I don't know how he managed to escape and find his way back. Clever Teddy!

"Who could have done that?"

By this time I was really exhausted and Teddy wasn't looking too wide awake either (but he smelt beautiful) so although it was only halfway through the day we cuddled up together and went right off to sleep for quite a long time. I have made up my mind though that Teddy must not come out to help dig the America tunnel any more, it's far too dangerous. In fact I think he should stay inside from now on; you never know what is going to happen and I need my Teddy.

10: A VERY UNHAPPY PUPPY

Well, since my last adventure I have had several visits to the nice vet. It is all that naughty Wilma Pumi's fault. You see, Wilma and I are only allowed to play outside together for a short time a couple of times a day as we get so excited and run around the garden so fast Mum is worried that I might get hurt. She calls us a pair of hooligans. Well a little while ago we were having our chasing game in the garden when Wilma suddenly stopped and looked at the undergrowth with her head on one side. I headbutted her to tell her to get moving but she just wouldn't budge, just kept tilting her ears, which are VERY big, backwards and forwards. Then suddenly she jumped into the undergrowth and nearly disappeared. I thought this must be a new game so I jumped in after her only to find a funny looking spiky creature rolled in a tight ball. Wilma was trying to roll it over so of course I did the same but the silly thing didn't want to play and just rolled up tighter, so I tried rolling it with my foot. No, that wasn't going to work either. By then Mum, who never leaves us out on our own together, had come to look and said LEAVE IT in a very loud voice. Wilma obeyed immediately but I am ashamed to say that sometimes I get so excited that I don't always obey straight away.

Next thing I knew I was being lifted up and carried into the house and put into my crate without a blanket! Wilma was put away too and Mum disappeared with her car keys. I didn't mind though as I settled down to have a really good scratch. Gosh I was itchy, I scratched and scratched and scratched. Mum was back in no time and lifted me on the grooming table and put something wet on the back of my neck. After that I felt okay for a while but in the night the itch came back so I had a good scratch again only this time it didn't seem to help much so I tried biting the places I could reach, that was better. My tummy was the worse so I bit at that too but somehow it just seemed to get worse. I was quite a sad puppy by the morning.

Mum took me to see the vet and I had an injection which she was told would do the trick and I was to go back in a week. I don't know what the trick was but it didn't work. My Mum cuddled me most of the day and I was put to bed that night on a cool pad and a towel but when my Dad got me up the next morning to take me out he could see that I wasn't a well boy, so he rang the vet and said I must see him that morning.

Back I went again. This time I was really hurting and I didn't want anyone to even look at my tummy but I tried to be a good boy and rolled over on my back. The nice vet man was very unhappy to see me so sore. He put cream on my tummy and inside my legs, and then I had another injection and two lots of tablets. Then, as if I hadn't had enough, he put a blue doughnut thing around my neck! It was to stop me biting or scratching myself. Then, at last Dad and Mum took me home.

I didn't really mind the doughnut and I am quite good at taking tablets as Mum has taught me that for every tablet I take I get one of my special Ruby Dooby Biccys. I didn't like the cream which was cold on my tummy but I knew it was for my own good so I let Mum put it on me twice every day. I had to wear that doughnut for two whole weeks and can you believe it, several people laughed at me. A friend of my Mum came to visit me and she started to laugh and then pretended she was coughing, huh! She said I looked as if I was waiting for someone to give me a pair of swimming trunks and a towel. Rude lady, I'll tell you what it is going to take a lot of grovelling from her and a huge amount of Special Ruby Doobys before she gets any more kisses from me.

Anyway the doughnut is off now, I have finished all my tablets and life is good again. Mum says I am a happy bunny once more.

That reminds me, as most people will know by now I am a very happy puppy. Everyone says so. And when I am really happy, I bark, I can't help it. Well, someone has written a song that must have been meant just for me. It has made me even happier. Mum and I were driving in the car the other day – well, Mum was driving as of course dogs, even ones as clever as Pulis, are not allowed to drive. I was sitting in the back watching the fields full of cows and sheeps go by when I suddenly realised what the man on the radio was singing. I don't remember all of the song but I think I have got the bit he kept singing over and over. It went like this:

Cos I'm HAPPY
Bark along if you feel like a room without a roof
(Silly isn't it?)
Cos I'm HAPPY
Bark along if you know that happiness is the truth
Cos I'm HAPPY
Bark along if you know that happiness is for you
Cos I'm HAPPY
Bark along if you feel that that's what you want to do
Cos I'm HAPPY.

Isn't that just terrific? He must be someone who knows me. I don't know what the song was called but feel sure it must be something like Rooster's Song.

11: I MEET NEW FRIENDS

The other day I decided that I really should do a bit more work on the America tunnel. Mum and Dad were going out for a couple of hours and as we can't get out of our garden they like to leave a door open so we can get outside if we need to or I can go out and play for a while if I get bored. I told daddy I was going into the garden to play a while and all he said was don't get into mischief, huh, as if I would!

Anyway I have been digging for a while now and I am pretty sure I was under the ocean as for a few days it was very damp down there, it is a lot drier now so I decided to start going up slightly and see if maybe I had reached America. I thought it strange that I hadn't met Teddy somewhere along the way. I hoped I hadn't missed him somewhere as my Mum and Dad were going to get a big surprise if he popped up in our garden. Anyway I set off down the tunnel until I reach the bit that still needed some digging and I set to it. Well I hadn't been digging long when bits of earth started trickling down on me, I knew it! I knew I was close! Then some grass fell on top of me and I got really excited and dug really fast. Suddenly, there it was, I could see the sky, America! I had reached it! I broke through and came up in a field of grass, just next to a hedge. I wondered why none of my Puli mates were there to meet me? Where were Teddy, Parker, Bruin, Edes and the others? Maybe I overshot Teddy's place? So where was I?

The last bit of digging had been quite tiring, so after shaking several times to get rid of the earth from my coat I sat for a minute to get my bearings and see if I could see anything to tell me where I was. Well I was in a big meadow, full of grass and lots of wild flowers, a few big trees but nothing else. I could see a wooden gate over in the far corner. It was all very quiet and obviously no one was going to meet me, so deciding I would go and see America for myself, I set off for the gate.

As I approached I could hear a bell ringing in the distance and somebody whistling so I popped through the gate and found myself standing in a small lane. Coming along the lane towards me was a man on a bicycle. He had a funny sort of flat black cap on his head, a black and white striped jumper and a big moustache. Even stranger than this he carried a long string of onions around his neck. He stopped and we both looked at one another for a moment, then he broke into a big smile. "Eh mon petit chien," he said, dropping his bike on the verge and kneeling beside me. "From where did you come? Are you lost?" Unfortunately, he seemed to be speaking another language and I didn't understand him, I had thought people in America spoke English? We looked at one another for another moment when he suddenly smiled even wider and said, in English "Ah, you do not understand the French, you are not a little French dog. Mon Dieu where then did you come from? Now, what do I do? I expect you require food and water yes? You had better marché along with me." Picking up his bike and starting to push, "Come, come now, follow me." He seemed a very nice man and I was very hungry and thirsty by now so I followed along.

Soon we arrived at a little cottage, with a goat and some chickens in the garden. Do you know, I was beginning to think this was maybe NOT America, something didn't seem right somehow. Anyway the man propped up his bike and calling "Maman, Elise, Etienne, come see what I have found." He entered the cottage. I followed him to find a lady dressed in a grey dress with a lovely white apron with frills around it and two children. The little girl jumped up "Papa, papa tu as trouvé un Chiot!"

"In English Ma Chou, in English, he certainly doesn't understand the French," said the man who I realised was called Papa.

"Papa, you found a puppy, he looks just like Beau. Can we keep him Papa, can we keep him, please?"

Meanwhile Maman had brought me a lovely dish of meat and biscuits and a big bowl of water, which I soon got tucked into. "Ah pauvre puppy," said Maman. "He is hungry, where did you find him Pierre?"

"In the big meadow, he just popped out through the gate."

"Please can we keep him Papa?" said Etienne. Papa looked at me for a while, I was getting a little worried as although they seemed to be really nice people, I was just visiting and wanted to go home to my Mum and Dad sometime.

"Well I don't know," said Papa slowly, "it seems to me that he must have come from somewhere and maybe somebody loves him very much and would like to have him back home with them."

"He has a collar on Papa," said Elise.

"So he has, well spotted Ma petit... Now let's have a look." Papa looked at my collar and read my tag "Mon dieu!" he exclaimed. "Le petit puppy comes from England. He is called Rooster."

"Rooster, Papa?" said Etienne? "As coq?"

"Oui," said Papa, "Rooster." The children giggled!

"But Papa, he is a puppy, not a chicken," said Elise.

"Now how did you get here?" said Papa almost talking to himself. "Let me think about this. There have been no cars by today, there are no trains around here, and you certainly could not have dropped from the sky. I think when I have had my dinner and we have rested a spell we will go and have a look around the meadow."

Maman brought Papa's dinner in for him and a big glass of some dark red stuff, then she noticed I had eaten all my delicious meat and biscuits and drank most of my water so she went back to the kitchen and brought me another bowl of each. After Papa had finished eating he took his boots off and put his feet up on the hearth and shut his eyes. Soon I could hear gentle snoring. It was almost soothing and as I was quite tired myself I stretched out and went off to sleep too. When I woke I saw that Papa was already awake and staring down at me, he put his hand down and stroked me for a minute, saying to Maman "Do you know when I awoke and saw him there it was just as if..."

"I know Pierre, I know," she said. "He is very like him, I know how much you miss him but he was a great age and it was his time. You will have another dog in time."

Papa blew his nose very hard then pulling his boots back on, he said to me "Come now we will go and have a look around the meadow." Calling the children to him we all set off down the lane, reaching the gate quite quickly. The children and I scrambled through but Papa opened it and walked into the field, carefully shutting the gate behind him. "Now Mon Petit Chien, what can you tell me?" he asked. I set off across the field with Etienne, Elise and Papa following me and soon came to the entrance to my tunnel. The children stared at it with open mouths and Papa sat down suddenly on the grass.

"It is a tunnel Papa, it is a tunnel," they shouted. "Le Puppy has dug a tunnel to come here."

"Mon Dieu, you are right," said Papa "all the way from Angleterre." He looked at me for a minute. "I don't know if I should tell you that you are a clever puppy or a foolhardy one, but one thing I do know is that you are a lovely, well behaved and well looked after puppy and clearly at the other end of this tunnel there is a family who loves you and will want you back. I think we must say goodbye and let you be on your way."

" Papa, Papa, no Papa please let him stay with us," cried the children.

"No he must go home to his family who will be very unhappy if they lose him," said lovely Papa.

"Say goodbye children."

The children knelt down to me and hugged me tight,

I gave them kisses and tried to tell them I would miss them. Then I went and put my paws on Papa's knees and looked in his eyes. "Au revoir mon petit," he said giving me a hug. "Remember us sometimes, we would have loved having you stay and live with us but you must go now back to your own people." Do you know I think he had tears in his eyes. I licked his face and it tasted all salty. I hesitated torn between staying or leaving but "Go now," he said. I turned reluctantly towards the tunnel. At the opening I stopped again and looked back over my shoulder, Papa's eyes were still wet but he was smiling. "Go now Bebe, go, Bon Voyage."

So I turned and headed back down the tunnel.

At first I felt really sad, as I walked along, they were such a nice family and I think I would have been happy living there with them. I did hope they found another puppy to live with them soon. Although I was sad I realised that the further I went the more excited I became. I picked up my pace and began to run. I was going home! Back to my Mum and Dad who I love and back to my mummy and daddy and the rest of my family. I was even looking forward to seeing Grumpy old Granny again.

Eventually I could see light coming through the tunnel and there I was in my own garden, as I made my way up the lawn daddy was sitting on the door step looking around for me. "There you are young Rooster," he said, "what have you been doing, you've been out here ages and Mum and Dad have just pulled into the yard? I hope you haven't been getting up to mischief!"

"Au revoir mon petit"

12: OBSERVATIONS

Mum and Dad have been on holiday this week with the bowls club and couldn't take us with them. Dad explained that everyone was going together on a coach so no dogs allowed. I do think I could have travelled on the coach, I am sure just about anyone would have loved to have me sit next to them and then I could have looked out of the windows at all the cows and sheeps in the fields. I would have enjoyed that. However they have promised that they will take us away for a few days in the car soon.

So this week we have had our lovely dog sitter who comes and lives in our house and takes care of us. She is a really super lady called Emma and she loves us a lot. We are always glad when she comes to stay with us. The only thing is she takes SUCH good care of us that I don't get chance to do so much adventuring. So this week I thought I would just put down some thoughts and observations.

Mum took me for a walk the morning before they went on holiday. We went to the place where she and Dad take all the big dogs for their walks. I haven't been able to go there before as I was not old enough for such a long walk. It's difficult to describe this special place but when you get out of the car there is a little lane up to a gate and once you are through the gate, wow! There are no fields or fences or hedges, no cars or roads, for as far as you can see. Just grass, bracken and hills, it's just magic. It was such a nice day that there were a lot of people walking the hills, Some of them had dogs with them but quite a few didn't and it got me thinking, Isn't that a waste of a good walk? Quite a few people had packs on their backs and big boots and sticks. One man even had a baby in his pack but *NO* dogs. Such a shame as I am sure there are loads of dogs who never go anywhere and would just love to be taken for a walk. If people don't have a dog of their own couldn't they find one to borrow? I am sure someone could sort that out if they gave it enough thought?

The best thing ever, when we started climbing up the hills was the smell, oh my goodness the scent was incredible. At first I couldn't work out what it was, it was like some wonderful memory that I couldn't quite recall. I was sure I should know it but try as I may, I just couldn't think. Mum laughed at me because, as I was on my running lead she said I looked like a scent hound as I ran backwards and forwards with my nose down trying to discover the source of that wonderful smell. Then, coming out of the bracken and heather, I saw them, *SHEEPS!* Up until now I have only seen sheeps from the car window but these two were walking towards us on a little path to the side. I was *SO* amazed I just stood and quivered. My instinct said Go, Go, Run, Chase but from somewhere deep inside me came a little voice that told me chasing stray sheep was not allowed. Mum confirmed this by saying quietly "No Rooster, leave". I sat down quickly in case my legs ran after the sheeps without me telling them to. We sat together and watched the sheeps walk right by us and away into the distance, until we couldn't see them anymore. I turned to my Mum with an amazed look and she told me I was a very good pup and gave me one of my special Ruby Dooby biccys she always carries with her.

Do you know in our town there is a machine in a wall that gives you money if you put a card in a little slot. I went with Mum today and there were a lot of people queuing to do it. When it was our turn I put my feet up on the wall to watch. I wonder where you can get that little card? If I can grow a bit bigger I am sure I could put a card in the machine and get money, not that I want any but I know humans like to have some and I could give it as a present to my Mum and Dad.

Why is it do you think that more than one cow is called cows, a bird is a bird until there are more than one then they become birds. It goes on and on, dogs, cats, rabbits... until you get to sheep! One on its own is a sheep, more than one and people still call them sheep. How silly is that? It clearly should be sheeps. I think one day long ago someone must have said "Oh look there is a sheep, and look there is another sheep", so eventually people forgot there was an S and just called them sheep. This is so obviously wrong and I think it should be put right so I am going to carry on calling them sheeps and I hope all you sheep dogs out there will join my campaign.

As those of you who know me know, I love going with Mum and Dad to watch sport. Bowls is my favourite of course but I also go with my Dad to watch football and that is a good game too and during the summer when Dad has a free afternoon he sometimes takes me and daddy Hank to watch a game called Cricket. What is that all about? The first time we went I watched for a while then asked my daddy who was snoozing in the shade, to please explain what was happening. "Don't ask me," said daddy. "We Americans don't understand Cricket." Fortunately an old Jack Russell who is always there said "Come over here son and I will explain it to you."

Well he took a long time to explain how it worked but I must admit that I got more and more baffled by Silly Mid Wickets, Googlys, Maidens Over and a load of other strange phrases. In the end I thought the best thing would be to just watch and try and work it out myself. So here is how I think it is played.

There are two teams who both wear white clothes so you don't know who belongs where. There is a long strip of short turf cut into the grass with little posts stuck into the grass at each end and then someone balances another post across the top. Big mistake I think as it is bound to fall off at some point. Then the man with the ball (and this *IS* a ball not a bowl although, strangely, the man is called the bowler) walks several miles away across the field then turns and runs back with his arm going round in a circle, faster and faster until he gets to the posts then he throws the ball very hard at the other posts. Unfortunately, standing in front of the other posts is a man with a bat and it seems to be his job to stop the bowler hitting the posts by giving the ball a swipe with his bat.

I do hope you are still with me?

After the man throws the ball, one of three things will happen. Firstly the man with the bat misses the ball and it hits the little posts straight on and the top post falls off. Sometimes the posts that are in the ground even fall over, which is no surprise as anyone can see they have not been hit into the ground far enough. Or the second thing that can happen is the ball hits the man with the bat, hard, on his leg, which must hurt but I don't really have any sympathy for him because it is a daft place to stand anyway and he is almost bound to get hit sometime! Or thirdly the man with the bat hits the ball and away it goes across the field usually with a couple of men chasing after it.

Now here is where it gets a bit complicated.

There is another man on the field who usually stands behind the posts. He is clearly a *VERY* important man and I think he also suffers badly from the cold as he always wears a long white coat and usually has several woollen jerseys tied around his neck too. Now, when the man who threw the ball hits either the posts or the man with the bat, all the men standing around explode – they jump up and down and shout something that sounds like *OWWSSZAATT* – then everyone looks at the important man and waits. He can then do one of two things. Either he can hold up just one finger, in which case the man with the bat looks very unhappy and walks off and all the other men look delighted and dance around a bit ... *OR* he can shake his head slowly and cross his hands back and forward in front of his knees, in which case the man with the bat stays where

"here is where it gets a bit complicated"

he is and all the other men stop dancing, look very sad and get on with the game. Now if Pulis are ever allowed to play cricket, I already know which position I want to play: *The Important Man!*

I think this explains it well enough for you to understand. One thing I should add though is that I say men all the time because I have only seen men playing but the nice Jack Russell who, by the way, is called WG, did tell me that ladies also play Cricket. Personally I always thought ladies to be far more sensible, but there it is.

13: A DAY WITH MY DAD

Mum was going out for the day, so she asked Dad if he wanted her to take me. "No," said Dad, "I have a lot to do in the garden today, he can stay and help me and then in the afternoon I will take him for a walk." Yippee, that's the kind of day I like best. I wondered if our walk would take us to the pub. I love going there, it's full of really nice people, mostly men, who sit around a table talking about people they think they remember from 'the old days' many years ago and arguing about what their names were. They all know me and give me hugs and feed me crisps and things. It's fun!

As soon as Mum left, Dad put on his gardening boots and picked up his tools. First job of the day was to get that bad green garden water snake out to water all of my Mum's pretty flowers. These live in pots and baskets and tubs and are very precious to my Mum and must not be allowed to get dry. Dad unrolled the snake from his home on the wall and walked off around the corner to start on the flowers. As I sat watching that nasty snake slither by me I remembered the men playing that tug of war at the show we went to a few weeks ago. I thought I could play a trick on my Dad. I waited until he had disappeared around the corner and I could hear the water, then I took a hard grip on the snake's middle bit and pulled backwards with all my strength! Ha, the snake stopped pulling for a minute but I just held on, then the pulling started again. I pulled it backwards once more and after a very little while it stopped again. This WAS fun. I waited for it to start again, Dad must be wondering what was wrong with it! Then I looked up and there was Dad just standing at the corner looking at me. Oh dear. I put down the snake and smiled at my Dad to show I was playing a joke. He smiled back and said "We are going to get a long way today like this aren't we? Now, leave it, good boy."

Okay, I had been rumbled. I thought I should go and play for a while and stay away from the snake. I went for a walk around the garden checking on what needed to be done when Dad had finished the watering. I did notice that the silly snake had got itself caught up around a tree stump but I knew I mustn't start pulling him again. All of a sudden I heard my Dad shout at the top of his voice *"ROOSTER!"* He then called something like 'leave it' but by then I was down the garden and halfway around the corner. That BAD snake must be attacking my Dad. I raced to rescue him. Sure enough Dad was standing amongst Mum's flowers holding the snake's neck – I was just in time! I jumped for the snake's head and we wrestled it together. Dad kept saying "No Rooster, leave it Rooster", but I know that was only because he didn't want me to get hurt, but I am a Puli, we are brave and *NO ONE* not even a dangerous snake was going to attack my Dad if I was there to save him. We wrestled the nasty creature for a few more minutes, there was water EVERYWHERE; we were both SOAKED. Dad must have been getting very tired because he dropped the snake and went off around the corner leaving me to deal with it. All of a sudden the fight went out of it and it stopped throwing water everywhere. I was not sure if it was dead or just exhausted but I was left standing, panting hard, dripping wet with a lifeless snake in my mouth. Whew, that had been touch and go for a while. Dad arrived back again and he was wet through too. I grinned at him and all of a sudden he started to laugh. "What am I going to do with you Rooster?" he said. "Look at us, we are soaked and we have only done one job so far."

We went back into the house and Dad dried me with a towel, then he changed his wet clothes so we were ready to start again. "Okay, next job bring up some wood chippings," said Dad, getting the wheelbarrow from the shed.

We set off down the garden and through the gate into the orchard. Now this place is still called the orchard even though daddy told me that all the old fruit trees had fallen down and been taken away a long time ago. Something to do with generations of Pulis digging deep holes under them. Hmm, I wondered where I got my love of digging! Anyway there are some new little fruit trees there now and we Pulis are not allowed in there unless someone is with us. There had been a man working in there a few weeks ago with a big, noisy machine, pushing the rest of the big old branches in one end and lots of little bits of the branches came flying out of the other. It was like magic! I had watched him for a while, he was a really nice man too. I sat with him and we had a bit of a cuddle while he drank the coffee Mum made him.

Anyway, Dad now wanted some of the bits of branches, which are called bark (Ha, funny) chippings, around the bushes in the yard. I barked at the wheelbarrow as Dad pushed it. Not because I am bothered by it, just because I like barking at it, but Dad picked me up and popped me in it! Wow that stopped me barking. I had to balance very hard as Dad is a bit wobbly with the wheelbarrow. When we got to the orchard gate I jumped out to help Dad open it. We got in a bit of a mix up with Dad pulling and me pushing but we finally sorted it out and pushed the barrow through. Now to load it up with the chippings, Dad set to work with his spade. I decided, not having a spade of course, that the best thing I could do would be to dig in the pile sending the chippings in Dad's direction. Sadly Dad didn't think much of this idea, and told me to stop immediately, apparently I was covering him in chippings, so I sat and watched him fill the wheelbarrow. When he thought he had enough he put down his spade and started to push the barrow off up the garden to the yard. I followed, wondering if I could risk jumping up on the barrow but deciding against it.

When we got back to the yard, Dad emptied all the wood chippings into a pile on the earth then went back to do the same thing again. We did this four times and I have to say I was getting a bit bored so the last time he went back I stayed in the yard. I studied the piles of chippings for a while, realising that dad wanted them spread over the earth to make it tidy. Well I could do that for him. I set to work on the first pile, digging hard and making the chippings fly out behind me and spread over the earth. I was almost finished the second pile when Dad appeared with his rake. "Rooster, what have you done?" I grinned, I could see he was pleased, I looked behind me at the job I had done when I saw that quite a lot, in fact most, of the chippings had landed not on the earth but on the tarmacked driveway. Oops, that wasn't meant to happen. I thought it best at this stage if I took myself off a bit so I went and lay down on the back step, far enough away to stay out of trouble but close enough to watch Dad first go and get the yard broom and a big shovel and sweep up the chippings from the driveway and throw them onto the earth. Then he took the rake and spread the rest over the earth in between the tubs and pots. I must admit it looked very tidy.

By now I was ready to get on with some more gardening but I wasn't too sure if Dad wanted me to help or not, so I stayed on the step but just as I was beginning to feel a tiny bit sad Dad called me to him. Of course he needed my help, silly me. We walked down to where he had previously cut some branches off the lower bits of the fir trees. They needed moving to the bottom of the orchard. Dad picked up a couple by their ends and started to drag them along. Easy, I could do that! I took hold of them too and pulled hard, most unfortunately it's quite difficult to see where you are going when your head is hidden by fir tree and it turned out I was pulling in the wrong direction so that wasn't going to work. Dad knew the answer though, he broke off a small branch and gave it to me so I followed him, pulling my very own branch along until we got to the big pile and he threw his big branches right up on the top. He was then going to put mine up there too but I held on tight, it was *MY* branch and I was *NOT* going to let go. We went back, me pulling my branch and Dad picked up some more big ones and we took them back to the pile. This WAS fun. After a while though I got a bit tired so I dropped my branch and Dad picked it up and threw it on the pile with his. While he finished up gathering the last branches I had a really good idea. As he pulled them off I ran and jumped on top of them. It was great fun, a bit like being pushed in the wheelbarrow but I was bumping along the ground. When we reached the pile Dad pretended he hadn't known I was there. "Oh Rooster," he said, "I thought these last branches were very heavy, I didn't know I was pulling a tubby puppy along too." I wagged my tail hard and jumped up for a cuddle. Yes you did Dad, yes you did!

Once Dad was finished with the branches he decided we had done enough gardening for that day so as it was lunch time we went inside and Dad gave me a small snack of my special Ruby Dooby biscuits, while he made a cup of tea and a sandwich for himself. I had a bit of a doze while Dad read the paper for a while. Then it was time for my walk. I love going out with Mum and Dad, I did my happy dance, just for a minute and then I stood really still to have my collar and lead put on, and out we went to the car.

Dad lifted me in and off we went. I always like this bit as I don't usually know where we are going, so it is a lovely surprise. This time as I watched out of the window I recognised the road, we were either going to the park or to the Bowls club. I didn't mind which as I like both but this time when I was lifted down we set off for the park gate. There is a really funny picture on the gate, which always makes me giggle, it is of a big white dog standing on his back legs using a pooper scooper. He must be really clever to be able to do that as I have tried it and it is not easy.

I am not yet allowed to go off the lead in the park as Mum and Dad worry that something, a big dog maybe, would frighten me and I would run away, so Dad attached me to my extending lead so I could run and play. We headed in the direction of the river; it's a good spot, you can paddle at the edge and watch the fish. As we arrived we could see some people having a good time trying to make stones bounce over the water. Dad recognised two of his friends who had come with their family, so we stopped to talk. I was fascinated by the stones and moved closer to the children who were playing there. I simply HAD to join in. Dad was busy talking and I could see that my lead was extended right out, so I waited for the next stone to go and *WHOOPI!* I launched myself after it. Straight into the water I went *SPLASH!!!!* The children laughed while I paddled around looking for the stone. Dad was not pleased. He guided me out by my lead and I gave a couple of good shakes, which got a lot of water over Dad and his friends. He did have a few severe words to say about me managing to get wet through twice in one day but his friend laughed and called me a 'character'. After that our walk got cut a bit short as I had to be taken home and for the second time that day I had to be dried off, only this time I was so wet I had to go in a crate next to the growly machine that blows the hot air. I don't like him at all but it was definitely worth it to have a lovely dip in the river!

14: ROOSTER TO THE RESCUE

The other day I was exploring the garden, collecting bits of stuff I wanted to keep, my Mum says clearing my mat is like emptying a small boy's pockets: pebbles, nuts, bits of wood, a slate, a pretty flower. I love collecting treasures. Anyway, I noticed something odd on the lawn and went to have a closer look. I found two baby birds. I am not sure how I knew they were birds as they didn't look like any I had seen flying around, they were small and pink and skinny, with no feathers, but somehow I was sure they were birds – I was also sure they shouldn't just be lying around on the lawn. Hmm, what to do???

I couldn't manage to pick them both up at once so decided it would be best to take one and then come back for the other. I picked one up and very carefully carried it inside and laid it down gently on my mat, it didn't look like it was going anywhere so I raced outside to get the other one. I was just carrying him in when Mum came out and asked me what I had got. Of course I couldn't tell her because my mouth was full of baby bird and I didn't want to put him down until I had got him safely inside on my mat. However, Mum insisted I give it to her, so I did. Funny, when she had it in her hand she didn't seem quite so keen.

By this time she had seen the first baby and called to my Dad who scooped them up and took them away. I hoped he was taking them to the nice vet who would make them better so I could have them back as my friends but they never came back. I keep a lookout now for any more and if I find any I will hide them until they are better and nobody can steal them from me.

15: A BUSY WEEKEND

It was a bank holiday weekend, I don't quite understand what that means but I do know that people have three days off from their work and things. It was also the finals weekend for my Dad's Bowls Club, I do know all about that because I go there a lot and listen to the people talking about things. Actually, I am quite proud because next season I am going to be their mascot and I am going to be made a social member, with a card of my own and everything! My Auntie Maureen has promised to make a tabard for me with my name and Official Team Mascot written on it. Won't that be something! I could be the only dog in the country who is the mascot for a bowls team.

Anyway my Dad was going to be very busy playing each day but Mum told him not to worry, as she and I would find lots to do.

So after I had my breakfast on Saturday, I had a bit of a doze while she tidied up and then it was on with my collar and into the car. "First stop," said Mum, "is Auntie Libby and Uncle Tim." I was really happy as I love them both and Auntie Libby always gives me treats. They live in a funny sort of little house called a Car a Van, or it could be a Caravan? I am not sure. Anyway I don't think they live there all the time as we only go to see them when it's the summer and once when we had lots of rain and wind, Dad took me there to check on things and it was all shut up and quiet. Well they were staying in their little house at the moment so off we went. They were very pleased to see me and gave me cuddles and I gave them Puli kisses. Then Uncle Tim went off for a walk to watch my Dad play Bowls for a while and Mum and I went inside with Auntie Libby. They also have three Pulis, a really nice old man dog who is gentle and kind like my daddy – he is called Ozzie – then there is my big sister Gaby who is lovely but a bit obsessed with food, then … there is *Tina!* Well, Mum says I mustn't write anything rude about anyone but Tina is *NOT* nice! She doesn't like me and says rude things and tries to bite me when no one is looking. She doesn't like Auntie Libby giving me treats or even touching me and growls things like "You get away you ugly puppy, she's *MY* mum". Charming! Anyway, we visited for quite a long time with Mum and Auntie Libby drinking coffee and talking (my Dad calls it gossiping) while I played with some of the toys that were in a box there. Every so often Tina came and snatched one off me saying "That's mine, that's mine", honestly you would think the whole world belonged to her!

After the coffee drinking had finished, we said goodbye and Mum put me in the car again. Tina muttered so only I could hear her "Good riddance and don't come back, ugly puppy, nobody wants you here."

Next stop was the Bowls Club where we dropped in for a while so everyone could have the chance say hello to me and so we could watch Dad play. Would you believe there was a very big, old Labrador and he was sitting beside *MY* bench. However, remembering how horrid Tina was, I was determined to be friendly so I stopped to talk to him. He was very nice and called me young'un. Fortunately I found out that he and his Dad were just visiting and had called in for a while to watch. I don't want to seem unkind but I am not used to seeing other dogs at my club.

We watched Dad win his game then set off again for a quick walk around the park. This was pretty uneventful today except I was really jealous of a couple of Terriers whose Mum was encouraging them to jump in the river after stones. I looked pleadingly at my Mum but she said "Not again Rooster, once was enough."

Back in the car and home again, I spent the rest of the day in the garden, collecting sticks and bringing them in for my Mum, playing with Teddy and digging a bit more of the America tunnel as I have now worked out were I had gone wrong before.

The next day was very exciting – Mum took Wilma and me to another show. This was a dog show but also a horse show. I have never seen so many horses in one place together. There were black, brown, grey and all sorts of mixed up colours. There were some REALLY big ones with lovely coloured ribbons in their manes and lots of shiny brass bits on their harnesses pulling huge carts, then some that were quite big and they were jumping gates in the middle of the field. Some being run along like a dog on a lead, with no saddles or bridles on, some small horses with little people riding them and some even smaller with tiny people sitting on them and being lead around by their Mums. It was really interesting. I was allowed to touch noses with one of the small ones which I now know are called ponies after the lady with him said he was very used to dogs. He sort of wuffled at me and his warm breath tickled my nose. It was lovely, I wish we had a pony.

It was soon time to leave the horses and head back to the dog show. We met Auntie Libby there and also my Auntie Jenny who is Mum to Dudley the Rot-something (I am still not sure what they really are called) that I had a play date with when I was a baby puppy. I was so looking forward to seeing him as I wanted to show him how big I am now and he wouldn't be able to push ME around. Oh boy, that was a mistake, I don't know what he gets for his tea but he is now HUGE, twice the size of me, but he was very friendly and glad to see me and we had a bit of a chat. Then the show started.

I was entered in 'The Handsomest Dog' and do you know what, I finally won one of those pretty ribbons, it was a lovely yellow colour, I think I was third. I was so happy with it, that Mum let me carry it out of the ring myself and I didn't drop it once! Some people sitting around thought I was very clever and looked and smiled and pointed at the cute puppy. One lady said to my Mum "He sure is proud of that."

When we got home, my rosette (that's what they are called) was given pride of place on the mantelpiece and I was given one of my Special Ruby Dooby Treats.

That's what I call a good weekend.

16: MY LAST QUESTION ANSWERED

Daddy called me in to the house today, he said he wanted to talk to me. He sounded serious and I had to stop for a minute to think if I had done anything naughty recently. No, I don't think so.

I hurried in to the house and found daddy sitting in the kitchen with mummy. My Dad was at work and Mum was upstairs with the thing that makes the carpets all clean and picks up all the dust.

"Sit down boy," said daddy "now, let me look at you. Hmm how old are you now?" I told him I wasn't quite sure. "He is 6 months," said mummy, "could I ever forget that long long…"

"Yes well," said daddy "no need to go into that again." He looked back at me for a minute. "Hmm six months? I think it's time we had a talk."

"Must you Hank?" said mummy. "Why don't you leave it for a while and see?"

"No, no," daddy said "the time has come."

Mummy sighed.

"Now boy," said daddy, "do you remember your brother and sisters leaving home?"

I nodded almost afraid to speak.

"Well, when we have a litter of puppies here, it is usually to keep one of the girls so when both your sisters left home it seemed to me that Mum and Dad were not going to keep a puppy this time. We waited for someone to come for you, but nobody did, did they?"

This time I shook my head, beginning to feel quite worried and sad, was my daddy going to tell me no one wanted me? Wasn't I good enough?

"Well," said daddy, "when you were still here after the others had gone, it occurred to me that you could be going overseas somewhere, like your older brothers Ethan and Dealer and your big sister Katie did some years ago. I even thought you could be going back to MY country." He closed his eyes for a moment as he always does when he thinks of America. "Anyway," he went on, "enough of that. It seems to me that if that was the case you would be gone by now and anyway I would certainly have been told as you know Dad shares everything with me..." He paused again just looking at me. "I can only think that you have been chosen to stay. I fail to understand why; Mum and Dad have NEVER kept a boy puppy before. Not in all the time I have been here. Why would they when they have me? It's a complete mystery. Clearly you are not as handsome as me." He drew himself up holding his head high and his tail tightly over his back. "And of course you will never have my presence. In fact you are a bit gangly and your tail has a distressing habit of wagging backwards and forwards and never staying in one place. Also you BOUNCE along instead of showing the beautiful, short stepping, smooth Puli action." He sighed loudly. "Still, you are my son and I suppose you show some promise. You will have to rid yourself of some airy fairy notions though, digging to America indeed, humph, in MY day we didn't—"

"Not now dear," said mummy.

"What? Oh right, anyway it seems you have been chosen to stay and carry on the family name, so be proud, behave yourself, obey Mum and Dad – and me of course – and try to live up to your name. Oh and by the way, one day I will be old and you will be young and strong but you WILL still respect me as I will still be in charge."

I waited several minutes but he seemed to have finished speaking so I asked if I could go now.

"What? Oh yes off you go," said daddy, "and remember all I have said."

"Oh I will daddy, thank you daddy." I raced off outside and did several laps of the garden at high speed. I just *HAD* to shout: I am staying, pretty flowers, I am staying rabbits. Look out, I am staying nasty green garden water snake, I'll be watching you, I am staying silly pigeons ...

I was staying, I was staying, I was going to be here for ever. I was *SO* happy, all I had to do was be good and not airy fairy, whatever that meant. Now, I had better do a bit more work on that America tunnel!

Lightning Source UK Ltd.
Milton Keynes UK
UKOW06f1817031215

264072UK00020B/973/P